Skiing for Beginners

Maurice Tugwell

with drawings by
Toby Buchan

Seeley, Service & Co · London

This book is for the Tod

First published in Great Britain 1977
by Seeley Service & Co. Ltd.,
196 Shaftesbury Avenue, London, WC2H 8JL

Copyright © 1977 Maurice Tugwell

ISBN 0 85422 138 7

Text set in 11/12 pt Photon Times, printed by photolithography,
and bound in Great Britain at The Pitman Press, Bath

Skiing for Beginners

Contents

Foreword

If you find skiing resistible, give this book to a friend. Learning to ski calls for a fuller measure of dedication, stamina and determination than half-hearted commitment can muster. The keenest beginner may experience moments close to despair; the reluctant or casual may wish he or she had stayed at home. Take my advice: stay home.

Unless the challenge is irresistible.

In which case, read on.

The advice which follows is non-expert advice. Expert skiers learnt to ski before they could walk. They lack comprehension of what it is like not to be able to ski; they cannot remember the frustrations and difficulties of learning; they have ample experience of skiing but insufficient understanding of our problems.

I first skied in my 40's. I found it difficult, sometimes baffling, often painful. I broke through. Now skiing is immensely enjoyable. Which does not make me an expert: it simply gives me pleasure. Because I can remember exactly what it is like not to be able to ski, and how difficult the simplest movements can be, I offer this book to help others break through to the superb enjoyment that skiing can offer. When you reach that stage and want to ski still better, consult an expert.

M.T.

The Scope of this Book

There are two forms of skiing: *downhill* or alpine, in which skiers start at the tops of mountains and finish at the bottoms, being carried back up again by machinery; and *cross-country,* Nordic, or Langlauf, in which skiers make their way across flat or undulating country enjoying the exercise, the scenery, and the benefit of actually getting somewhere. Techniques and equipment differ considerably. This book is concerned only with downhill skiing.

Downhill ski instruction can be divided into two main types—traditional and GLM (Graduated Length Method). In the traditional method students are fitted with skis of suitable lengths for their heights, and progress from elementary through intermediate and on to advanced lessons on the same skis; in the graduated length method students begin by learning intermediate or even advanced techniques on tiny skis, and progress onto sub-standard and then onto standard length skis. This method enables elementary and some transitional forms to be omitted altogether. In France GLM is called *Ski Evolutif.* GLM can only be applied in ski schools specially stocked with training skis of all lengths, and for the time being, at least, the majority of beginners will learn the traditional way. This book is for them.

Learning to ski involves

    some risk of injury
    at considerable expense
    coupled with exertion and frustration
    and frequent loss of dignity

        so why ski?

Because

    the atmosphere is invigorating
    the challenge, for many, is irresistible
    once you can stay upright, the sport is sensational
    and the sensation's out of this world

        that's why.

Chapter I

Skiing

GETTING READY

Instruction

You cannot learn to ski from a book, not even this one. You can reduce the time and agony of learning by combining practical lessons with book study. If you read this before your first experience on skis, *and think about it,* you will find the instruction easier to follow. If you read it between lessons it may answer questions which have puzzled you on the slopes, and it will *concentrate your mind* on the things that matter.

Your ski instruction may be in a class of eight or ten beginners under one instructor. This is the typical ski school arrangement. It works well enough, provides lots of laughs and a spirit of camaraderie, and is relatively economical. Its drawbacks are that the quick learners are apt to be held back and the less talented left behind, and that more often than not only one student in the class is actually doing any skiing. Far more flexible is private tuition, either for one individual or for two or three beginners of similar aptitude. This costs more, but the concentrated personal attention will advance your skill more quickly. Finally you can learn by the informal process of picking it up with a little bit of help from your friends. This is recommended only if you have a really devoted, reliable friend with a flair for teaching, who is prepared to give up a lot of his or her holiday to your instruction. A robust personality can learn after a fashion without an instructor, but is likely to develop bad habits without realizing it. If you have to learn like this, be sure to take a private lesson after three or four days to correct your faults.

Whenever you think you are doing all right, read the next chapter in this book and prepare yourself mentally for the next physical challenge. Whenever you are depressed by failure (and you'll be lucky if you never feel this way), read again from the start and identify the causes of your temporary difficulty.

This book will help: your instructor will teach. But only YOU can learn to ski. Ultimately it is your determination versus gravity.

Gear

Extravagant gear on a beginner looks rather absurd. Equip yourself adequately, not lavishly. Rented skis, poles and boots are OK, provided the latter fit really well and support your ankles. The ski bindings should be adjusted for easy release while you are learning, to be tightened a shade as you get more proficient. Warm and waterproof clothing, goggles and gloves complete your gear. Protect your face against sunburn. Don't learn on skis that are taller than you are, unless you enjoy doing things the hard way. Do not be intimidated by the ski rental folk. If you want more comfortable boots or shorter skis, insist. Shop staff are apt to bully beginners: remind them who is paying, and hold out for what *you* want. When you ski well enough to know what equipment suits your needs you may consider buying. Some advice on purchasing appears on page 63.

Skis

A pair of skis is composed of the skis proper (or boards, as irreverent Americans are apt to call them) and the bindings. The front of each ski curves upwards and is called the tip, and the back is known as the tail. Along the lower parts of each side is a metal strip which is the 'edge'. Laid flat, a ski touches the surface at two points only—one being several inches back from the tip, the other an inch or two forward of the tail. Between these two contact points the unweighted ski arches upwards: this arching is known as the bottom camber. With your weight on the ski it lies flat on the snow and the camber has the effect of spreading your weight along its entire length. The under-surface of the ski is called the sole. To promote straight and steady running, a groove is let into nearly the full length of the sole. The bindings are screwed into the upper surface so that the ball of the skier's foot is midway between the two contact points. Bindings usually consist of one gadget to secure the toe of the boot and another to clamp the heel flat onto the ski. Designers have to provide for rigid contact right up to the moment during a fall when the pressure from the ski threatens to damage an ankle or leg, and for clean and reliable release at that moment. They do pretty well. Because skis come away from boots when necessary, the two are connected by safety straps.

You must never allow a ski to career downhill on its own—it is a lethal missile. A safe way to park your skis until you need them is to shove them, tails first, vertically into the snow. When the time comes to fit them you must lie them flat on the snow, and here it is important to guard against their running away. This calls for an ability to judge something termed the *fall line,* to which we will be referring often in this book and which is an imaginary line running directly down the slope from where you are standing.

Now, take one ski at a time and place it at ninety degrees across the fall line, so that tips and tails are at the same height and there is no tendency for the ski to slide downhill. If necessary, push the uphill edge into the snow so that the ski is level in the lateral plane too. Fit the downhill ski first since this will assist your stability while you fit the other one. Remove snow and ice from under your boots, ensure that they are accurately centred between the bindings and make fast boots to bindings. Secure the safety straps, checking at the same time that your boots have remained correctly done up. Wear gloves always: they protect your hands against abrasion, as well as against cold and damp. Thrust your hands upwards . .

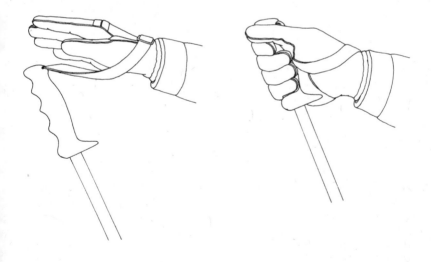

... through the straps on your poles ... and you are ready.

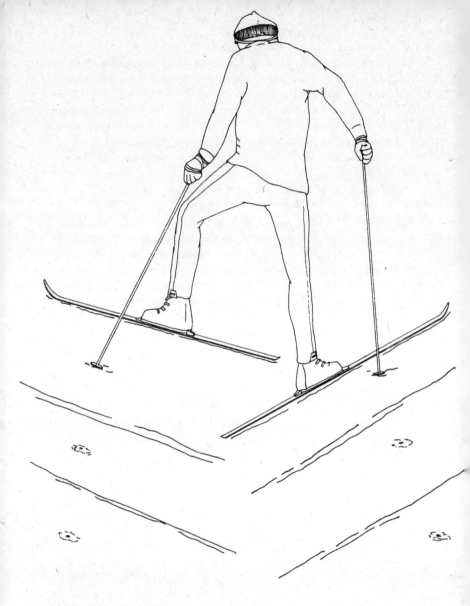

Getting up the Slope

If your slope is too steep to walk up—which is the case when your skis slip backwards on each step further than you have pushed them forwards—you have to either:

Herring-Bone your way up, by opening your skis ahead of you, at the same time turning the inside edge of each ski downwards, so as to grip the snow, the turn being known as *edging*

FALL LINE

or *Side-Step* up the hill by turning your skis across the fall line, edging into the hill, and shuffling up sideways.

It's difficult to say which is the more exhausting; console yourself with the thought that you are strengthening skiing muscles. After your first couple of lessons you will take a lift to the top of the nursery slope.

'Button' tow lift

Lifts

Your first lift is likely to be a tow, which skis you up the hill with the aid
of machinery. Tow-bars require you to hold a wooden baton which hauls
you along: anchors are designed for two skiers to be taken up side-by-
side each with half the 'anchor' behind the tops of the legs: buttons are
solo devices that fit between legs to pull skiers up in the same way. There
are other, less common, types. In all these tow-lifts the bar, anchor, button, or whatever, is connected to a moving overhead cable that provides
momentum. Take a good look at the apparatus on first acquaintance and
observe how others cope; there's nothing to be afraid of and soon you'll
treat the tow-lift like a moving staircase.

When your turn comes, make sure that your skis are parallel and
pointing up the hill, that your body position is relaxed and ready for a jerk

(skiing position, with knees and arms bent—not leaning forward with your bottom stuck out) and that your ski poles are not going to get in your way (take advice, according to the lift type). Look at the track about five yards ahead and, when your departure is imminent, shuffle your skis a shade forward. Between the cable and the bar, anchor or button there is a spring shock-absorber. When your tow device is engaged with the moving cable the spring stretches; then, as you start to move, it contracts, jerking you into motion. Next it expands again to its natural length for your weight and you are therefore liable to slow down after the initial acceleration. Be ready for the second slight jerk. Now you will proceed smoothly.

If your tow device is the type that you place behind your bottom, allow it to pull you comfortably up the hill. But keep your body weight on your skis—do NOT try to sit on the device.

In the unlikely event that you fall, let go of the tow device at once. Immediately roll, shuffle or slide CLEAR OF THE TRACK. Pick up the pieces and try to do better next time. Look at the whole business this way: all you are required to do is to adopt a skiing position and keep your balance on your skis while going up the hill. The tow device is simply your means of defying gravity.

Chair-lifts and gondolas, not to mention telecabines, make ascending simpler. Getting on and off chair lifts deserves study of those ahead of you, but is really quite easy.

A

B

CONTROL

Skiing out of control is not really skiing at all: it is plunging down a mountain with skis on your feet.

This warning applies from the day you begin and throughout your entire ski career. Always strive to ski under control.

Standing Still

On any but the gentlest of slopes, you need to turn sideways to the fall line, edge into the hill and stand upright with more than half your weight on the *downhill* ski. You will spend quite a lot of time in this position, initially during lessons, and later, waiting for your friends to catch up with you during a descent!

If you want to face the other way, do a *kick turn*. Swing your body partly round so that you face down the hill. Plant your downhill pole well back towards the tails of your skis and the uphill pole near to the tips (A). Shift all your weight temporarily onto the uphill ski at the same time supporting yourself with both poles. Now swing the downhill ski forward and up (B), until its tail rests on the snow: next swing it through 180 degrees, pivoting on its tail (C). When it is safely grounded (D) transfer all your weight to it and lift the uphill ski round so that it becomes the downhill ski (E). Shift more than half your weight to it and relax.

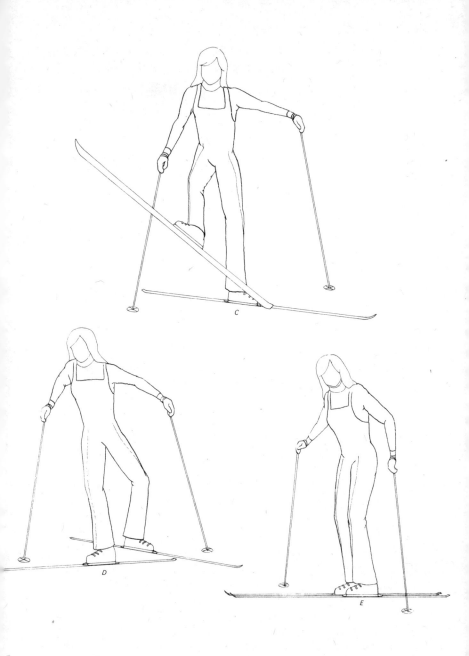

This kick turn is useful during instruction and it will be invaluable later, getting you down slopes too steep for your current ability to turn on the move.

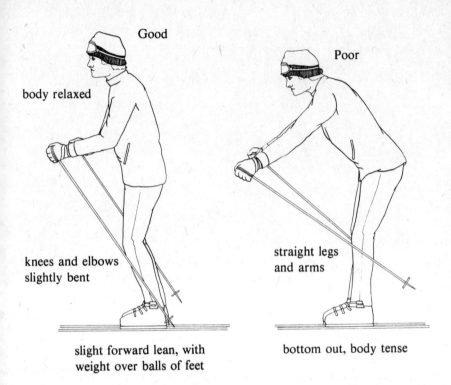

Good

Poor

body relaxed

knees and elbows
slightly bent

straight legs
and arms

slight forward lean, with
weight over balls of feet

bottom out, body tense

Skiing down the Fall Line

On a gentle slope terminating on flat snow, face yourself straight down
the fall line. You may shove your poles into the snow ahead of your feet
to prevent forward movement until you are ready to go (but you *never*
use poles in this way to halt movement). Allow yourself to move and
enjoy your first experience of skiing. Lean a little forward, knees and
elbows slightly bent, arms close to the body, hands about level with
jacket pockets, trailing the poles behind you, tips lifted just clear of the
snow. Do it again—several times.

If you are faced with calamity on one of these initial runs, such as imminent collision, relax your muscles and allow yourself to fall sideways
and slightly backwards onto the snow. It won't be the last time you will
fall, but this exercise is the last in which you are permitted to ski out of
control.

Skiing straight like this is called a *Schuss*.

14

Getting Up

Now that we have admitted to the possibility of falling, some advice on getting up. This is one of the few actions that is easier on a steep than on a gentle slope. Swivel round on your back until your legs are downhill of your body and then lower your skis so that they are on the snow at 90 degrees to the fall line. If the slope is steep you will be almost upright already and a push with arm or ski pole will right you. If the slope is gentle, more pushing is required, so bring both arms and poles into use. If necessary, both poles can be held in the downhill hand leaving the other one free to 'climb up' the poles as you raise your body off the snow.

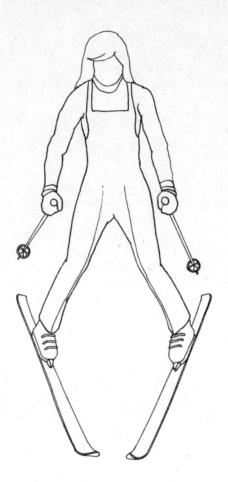

Stopping

The simplest method of controlling the speed of your decent and of stopping altogether is the *snow plough*.

Snow ploughing is a graceless and tiring movement, particularly for adults, and you will be glad to discard it as soon as you can. Nevertheless you will find it vital during your first week or two, since it provides *control* of speed and direction and thus permits the growth of confidence and ability. To me, as a student skier, it was what a baby-walker is to a child learning to walk—a means to an end.

To snow plough, bend your knees, keeping your weight central and keep the tips of your skis about three inches apart, while splaying the tails outwards as far as they will go. This is known as stemming. Edge both skis inwards. This requires steady, determined pressure from the thighs, legs and ankles, and you must keep your body low (which means bending

16

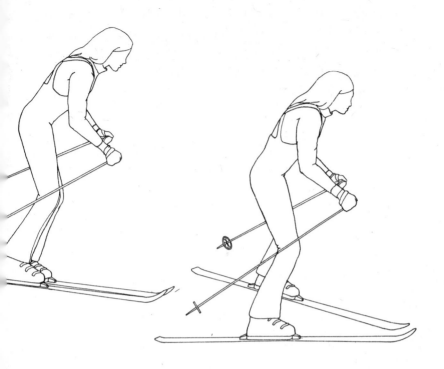

the knees) to apply sufficient force. You cannot snow plough properly if you ski stiff-legged. Some people find it helpful to think of a real mechanical snow plough and to imagine that they too are trying to scrape a clean path through the snow. By varying the pressure and the degree of edging, you can proceed straight down the slope at a perfectly controlled pace and you can *stop* exactly when you require.

You are skiing under control.

Practise complete runs in the snow plough position, varying your speed and finally stopping. Practise emergency stops, with a friend or instructor telling you when. Practise changing from schuss to snow plough position to check your speed, and from schuss to snow plough to stop.

Master the snow plough at this early stage and you are all set to succeed. Those who merely stem and edge their skis by pushing with their legs straight aren't going to get anywhere. Their control will be incomplete and their capacity to advance in subsequent lessons will be handicapped.

17

SKIING TERMS USED SO FAR

BINDINGS	attachments fixed to skis which hold skiers' boots in place but which release under excess of pressure.
BOTTOM CAMBER	the arch along the sole of the ski.
DOWNHILL	the direction in which the slope drops away from the skier (downhill ski, downhill arm, pole, etc).
EDGE (noun)	metal strip running the length of a ski on the lower parts of both sides that bites into snow or ice better than the material forming the ski itself. The inside edges are on the same side as the big toes, the little toes being by the outside edges.
EDGE (verb)	to force the ski against the snow at an angle, to grip the snow or to brake. 'Edge into the hill'—angle both skis so that their uphill edges bite; 'Edge both skis inwards'—angle each (stemmed) ski so that its inside edge bites.
FALL LINE	the line of most direct descent down a slope from wherever you are.
GROOVE	the shallow channel running nearly the length of a ski's sole.
HERRING BONE	a method of climbing uphill in which the ski tips are splayed and the skis edged inwards.
KICK TURN	a turn executed in a stationary position, the skier lifting first one and then the other ski through 180 degrees.
POLES	the ski sticks carried by skiers to assist control. At the pointed ends there are discs (or baskets) two or three inches up from the points, which limit depth of snow penetration.
SAFETY STRAPS	leather or fabric straps attached to bindings which clip or buckle round the skier's ankles.
SCHUSS	skiing more or less straight down the fall line, weight evenly distributed between skis.
SIDE STEP	a method of climbing uphill with the skis at 90 degrees to the fall line, and parallel.
SNOW PLOUGH	a method of skiing in which the tails are splayed outwards with the tips remaining close together, the skis thus forming a V.
SOLE	the lower surface of a ski.
STEM	the action of splaying out the tail of one or both skis.
TAIL	the trailing end of the ski.
TIP	the front, upturned end of the ski.
UPHILL	the direction in which the slope rises up from the skier (uphill ski, uphill pole, etc).

TURNING

The Art of skiing is the art of turning, and the art of turning consists of shifting your weight onto the correct ski. It is simple to understand in theory but it takes a little time and effort to put into practice.

Shifting your Weight

Remember how, when standing still on the slope, you stood upright with more than half your weight on the downhill ski? You felt secure and relaxed. If you had leaned your body too far into the hill, and especially if you had shifted your weight onto your uphill ski, your skis might have slipped downhill from under you and you would have fallen. If on the other hand you had leaned your body outwards away from the hill your stability would have increased, since the effect would have been to force your skis, and especially the weight-bearing downhill ski, into the snow. You will almost certainly find this easier to believe in theory than in practice. Once you are on a slope and feel in need of comfort, ten to one your instincts will tell you to lean into the hill. They will be misleading you; lean out.

You have experience, in the snow plough, of skiing with your two skis *stemmed,* that is to say pointed inwards in different directions. So long as you kept your weight central between your legs you progressed in a direction midway between the two skis. If you shift the bulk of your weight onto one ski, that will effectively determine the direction in which you will travel. In the snow plough, your left ski is pointing to the right and your right ski is pointing to the left. So if you shift your weight, or most of it, onto your right ski your whole body will start to turn in the direction your right ski is already pointed, to the left. As you turn to the left so your right ski becomes the downhill ski. That's good, because you already have most of your weight on it, and that means you have stability. Better still, to put weight onto the right ski you had to lean your body in that direction. So you finish your turn with your weight on the correct ski and your body leaning outwards from the slope.

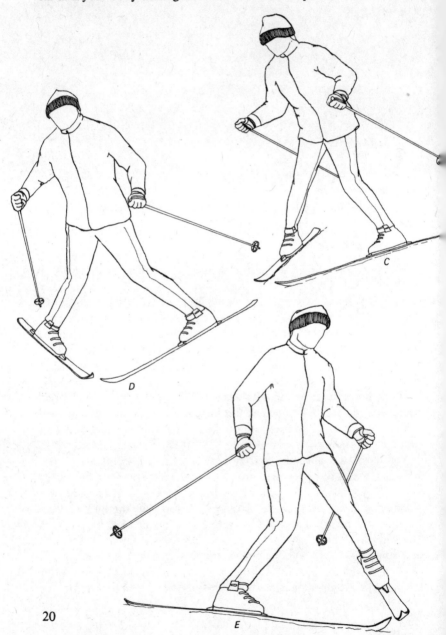

The Snow Plough Turn

Set off down the fall line in the snow plough position, A, easing your edges till you have reasonable speed. Now, to turn *right,* lean over the *left* ski, B, so that it is taking most of your weight. As you feel yourself turning, *keep leaning to the left* and round you'll go. It's quite extraordinary that the weight shift should actually turn you—but it does. Now do a turn to the left by leaning over the right ski, C. Really press on that ski. Round you'll go, D and E.

Linked Turns

Once you have mastered single turns, progress to a series of turns down the length of the slope. Remain in the snow plough position, control your speed according to how steep the slope is and how fast you want to go. Lose excessive speed prior to each turn and try to glance round just before turning, to see that the piste is clear. Use your emergency stopping capability as necessary. Throughout, ski under control.

PROBLEMS AND ANSWERS

P1. Falling inwards towards the slope at the conclusion of the turn.

A1. You are shifting your weight at the last moment onto the uphill ski. Very common; very understandable: don't do it.

P2. Difficulty in turning at all, or turns which straighten out almost at once.

A2. You may have a subconscious reluctance to committing your weight to the ski which, as you turn, becomes the downhill ski. Most of us at the beginning feel safer leaning into the hill, rather than out, for reasons with which we can all sympathize but which we must reject on scientific grounds. What you may be doing is pushing outwards on the ski which ought to accept your weight, while really retaining your bulk over the other ski. Think it out and start again.

P3. Gathering excessive speed during the turn, and crashing.

A3. Your basic snow plough technique is faulty. You gather speed, then, as you panic, you transfer weight to the uphill ski. You should have the same complete control over your speed whether you are turning or not. Are you bending your knees? Stiff legs often gather unwanted speed. Go back to straight snow ploughs and then, when these are satisfactory, retain the same control while you introduce turns.

If you can descend a slope in complete control of speed and direction, you can ski!

Why?

The text explained how, by shifting most of your weight forward and onto one of your stemmed skis, you moved in the direction of that stemmed ski. This is sufficient to explain how the turn begins. But why, you may ask, do you continue to turn so long as you hold your position, instead of just following the line of the ski?

The answer has to do with friction between the sole of your ski and the snow beneath it. Here you are doing your snow plough turn.

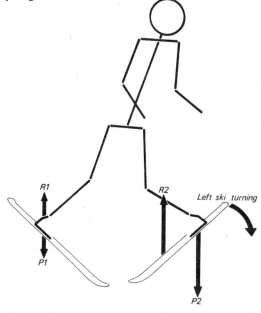

By weighting your left ski you have increased P2 (your propelling force) relative to P1. This will get you turning. Because your weight is forward , R2 (resistance) under the left ski is forward of P2 and these two components form a turning moment which continues to turn the ski as it moves.

This explains why I stress the need to bend the knees and get weight forward.

This principle applies equally in stem and parallel turns. All 'skidded' turns rely upon friction under the front part of skis.

PISTE	a hard-packed prepared ski run, frequently indicated with marker flags.
SNOW PLOUGH TURN	a method of turning in which the skier's weight is shifted onto one ski, while in the snow plough position.
WEIGHT CHANGE (or SHIFT)	the movement of the skier's weight from one ski to another, or from both skis onto one.

Chapter II

Skiing Properly

PROGRESS

It took me, in a class of ten, most of my first week to achieve reasonable proficiency in descending a gentle slope in a series of snow plough turns. It took my ten-year-old son two and a half days to reach a rather better standard. Do not be downhearted if you are a slow learner. I do not believe that the speed of assimilation bears much relationship to your eventual skiing ability. It could be that a slower and more painful trial and error apprenticeship preserves one from later setbacks.

In achieving the first level of proficiency (the ability to descend a gentle slope under control) and during the progressions which lie ahead, your capability rests upon two mutually dependent ingredients—confidence and technique. Like bricks and mortar, they are in turn raised up and in turn support each other. Since you begin your skiing without any technique, it follows that you need a measure of confidence founded upon determination if you are to get going at all. Hence in the Foreword my discouragement of halfhearted beginners. Once your technique develops it boosts your confidence and this enables you to tackle fresh challenges. Try to keep these two advancing in step. If your confidence lags, you are unlikely to succeed in mastering new techniques; build it up by polishing movements which are within your grasp. If your confidence outstrips your ability, beware the crash; try a difficult but not too dangerous manoeuvre and bring it down a peg or two.

When at the end of the last chapter we said that we could ski, this was true up to a point. The point is passed the moment our ambition or pride requires that we should *ski properly*. By this I mean the ability to leave the gentle slopes and attack the mountains—to attempt, however slowly, more challenging descents.

TRAVERSING

Your first important breakthrough in learning to ski was fearlessly shifting your weight from one ski to another, and keeping it so placed during and after a turn. The next major advance will occur when you get the knack of manoeuvring your skis with the help of a *down-up* motion of the body which enables you to turn quickly and easily on steeper slopes. I'll come to that presently. First, let us consider ski tactics on real mountains.

Schussing down is more often than not out of the question and the skier must descend by zig-zagging, keeping his angle of descent shallow enough to be within his skiing ability. Each zig or zag, that is to say each run across the slope between turns, is called a traverse, and the skier is *traversing*. This is a lovely movement, and when you try it you will probably agree that, for the first time, you are *skiing properly*.

The Traverse

Adopt the stance described earlier for standing across the fall line. Now relax into a good skiing position and point your skis downhill sufficiently for movement. Keep more than half your weight on your downhill ski, advance the uphill ski four or five inches ahead of the downhill, and edge into the hill to prevent side-slipping. This edging will automatically keep your knees in towards the hill. The upper parts of your legs should be upright and, to promote stability, lean your body, above the hips, slightly outward down the hill at the same time turning it about twenty degrees towards the fall line. This is the sexy S-shape position so often portrayed on ski posters. It is efficient and comfortable, and worth bothering about

Traversing Stance

because this *angulation* of the body to the skis becomes increasingly important as your skiing improves.

You can traverse along a trail or across a wide open slope and, adjusting your edges to suit conditions, you can feel perfectly confident traversing quite steep inclines. Of course the moment you lack confidence you will probably lean into the hill, your skis will lose their purchase and you will slide down the mountain like a beetle on its back.

Stopping from the Traverse

To stop traversing, all you need do is to return your skis to the standing still angle of ninety degrees to the fall line; in other words, stop pointing them downwards. You will have no difficulty doing this gradually, just by adopting a more forward lean. But in order to ski under control you have to be able to stop suddenly, exactly when you wish. This is how.

Traverse at a reasonable speed. Bend your knees and then straighten them, moving your weight forward, at the same time pushing your heels

Why?

Why lean out from the slope when traversing?

Because there is a force P which is trying to pull you sideways down the slope. This can be overcome by force R (resistance to motion, or friction), but only if R is equal to or greater than P. See how these two skiers cope:

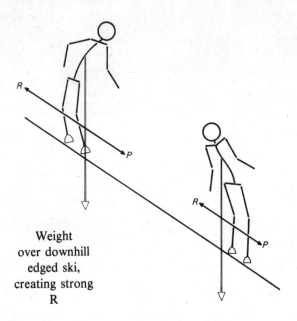

Weight
over downhill
edged ski,
creating strong
R

Weight
uphill of edged skis,
producing insufficient
R

down the hill. Your skis, still parallel, will swivel and point slightly up the hill, bringing you to an abrupt halt. You are already bearing more than half your weight on your downhill ski; be prepared for a sudden increased strain as you skid to a stop, but keep your weight on that same ski. As soon as forward movement ceases, adjust your skis to ninety degrees to the fall line, to prevent you from sliding backwards down the hill.

This is a knack. Keep trying until you master it. If you wish, use kick turns to change direction after each traverse. Once you have the knack you have taken an important step forward: you have discovered the value of the down-up motion, and you have made a start at *parallel skiing*.

Why?

Why does a forward lean help one to stop from a traverse?

Because, provided your skis are edged, when you move your weight forward there is an increase in resistance (R) forward of the bindings and a reduction of R at the tails. The force down the slope (P) and R form what is called a couple—two equal and opposite parallel forces acting on a body—and the tails therefore slide downhill faster than the tips.

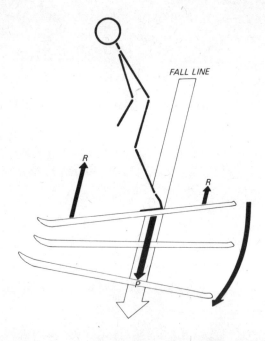

A backward lean has the opposite effect. R is increased rearward of the bindings and the tips descend faster than the tails.

FRESH TERMS

ANGULATION the body's lateral position in relation to the skis, often involving ankles and knees inclining inwards to the hill or towards the centre of a turn, while the body above the hips leans in the opposite direction to keep weight on the downhill or outside ski.

DOWN–UP the vertical bending or flexing of hips, knees and ankles followed by stretching or straightening up.

PARALLEL SKIING a technique of skiing in which the skis are kept parallel throughout all manoeuvres. The method was first practised by the Norwegians and took the name Christiania (the old Oslo) accordingly; 'christie' is short for Christiania.

TRAVERSE a descent running across the fall line of the slope.

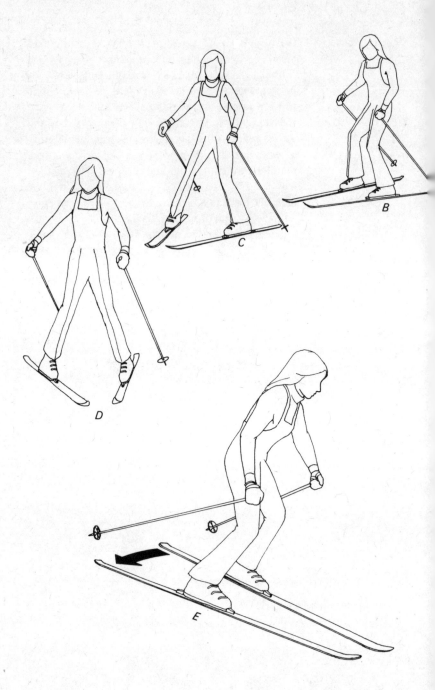

STEM TURNS

A

In learning to traverse and to stop we have mastered the zigs and the zags of our downhill descent. Now we want to join these up to zig-zag; in other words we must turn on the move from one traverse to the other.

You can use your snow plough turn, and in the early stages this will do quite well. The limitations of this method of turning become apparent as the slope gets steeper and as your speed in the traverse increases. On your zig and your zag you are skiing parallel: you need a turning method that will do two things:

a) Switch you, under control, from one traversing position to the other with (if this is your wish) the minimum loss of speed.
b) So far as possible eliminate the precarious moment (which seems like hours) when your turn faces you directly down the fall line of a steep slope.

Such a method is the *Stem Turn*.

In its basic form the stem turn is a smooth and fast derivative of the snow plough turn. In its advanced form as a stem christie, the turn makes

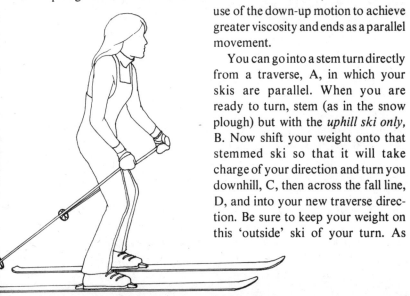

F

use of the down-up motion to achieve greater viscosity and ends as a parallel movement.

You can go into a stem turn directly from a traverse, A, in which your skis are parallel. When you are ready to turn, stem (as in the snow plough) but with the *uphill ski only*, B. Now shift your weight onto that stemmed ski so that it will take charge of your direction and turn you downhill, C, then across the fall line, D, and into your new traverse direction. Be sure to keep your weight on this 'outside' ski of your turn. As

33

you turn, inwardly edge your weighted, outside ski: this makes for stability and helps you to turn. After you pass the fall line and swing into your new direction, E, lift the unweighted 'inside' ski a shade and bring it alongside the one carrying your bulk so that you are parallel again for the next traverse, F.

Once you are confident about the basic stem turn, progress by introducing the down-up motion at the start. Go down as you stem the uphill ski and rise up as you bring the unweighted ski parallel. No need now to wait till the turn is almost complete before bringing that ski alongside: you can advance the return to parallel skiing by completing your down-up motion before you pass the fall line. Turning power, initiated by the stem, is now maintained by the turning effect of your edged outside ski and by the fact that your weight is well forward. This calls for a forward sink of the body after skis return to the parallel, and for knees to be pressed forward, and sideways into the turn.

As your down-up motion at the start of each stem christie develops a quicker rhythm, you will discover that the stemming is no more than a means to trigger off what is thereafter a glorious parallel turn: hence the title. The great joy of this turn is that it opens up to you descents which would have given you the willies in your recent snow plough days. You are turning across the fall line so fast and confidently that the awful fear that you might lose control at the critical moment and go careering off into the valley is banished.

In the stem christie your poles are brought into action. At the moment that you stem and bob down, 'plant' the downhill pole beside the forward part of your downhill ski. You start to turn around that pole, which gets pulled clear at about the moment your skis become parallel again. This takes a bit of coordination, so concentrate first on the ski movement. Then, on a familiar slope, try the same turns using the pole. You seldom have to think about lifting the pole clear: it just happens automatically as you overtake it.

Practise till it all falls into place (as a change from *you* falling into place). Once you can utilize the down-up motion to transform your stem into a christie, with your parallel skis making such a lovely noise on the snow, you have broken through to proper skiing. Test it on steeper slopes. If you are doing it correctly your confidence will soar.

Maybe you will be brought back to earth by discovering that, on the steepest part of your slope, just when you need quick turns most, the method fails you. This was my shattering experience. On thinking about it, upside down in the snow, I was suddenly confronted with the truth: instead of the method failing me, I had failed the method. Alarmed by the gradient, I had allowed my subconscious fears to gain control of my body. My legs had stiffened; I had not performed the down-up action; I had transferred my weight onto the stemmed ski only half-heartedly. Chastened, I tried again. Confidence subdued but consciousness restored, I did what I had been taught. It worked.

Falling

Learning to ski involves falling. Even an experienced skier will fall from time to time when pushing him or herself to the limit, or trying something new, or just by mischance. You, as a learner, must never be emotionally upset by physical upset.

A more subtle danger lies in the path of the learner who finds falling easy. The danger is that he or she adopts the fall as an easy way out. By falling as soon as a manoeuvre becomes alarming—and most techniques seem this way to the novice—this beginner subconsciously opts out of perceived danger by *not really trying to succeed.*

No real progress can be made unless the learner summons up the determination to really try—and this means making a conscious effort to stay upright throughout the entire movement.

In summary—fall as often as you must, but not as a deliberate escape from trying.

GOOD-BYE TO SNOW PLOUGHING

Your technique and confidence will advance in step as you *enjoy* your new-found freedom to ski under control down the slopes that seemed horrifying only days ago. You hardly ever use the snow plough now since your traverses are parallel, you know how to swing into the hill to stop, and you have polished your stem christies so that you can flick round corners. The few occasions when you still find the snow plough essential are likely to include:

a) When descending a narrow slope, across which you have insufficient room to zig-zag by traversing, but which is too steep to schuss down.
b) Stopping at the end of a schuss, when you are skiing directly down the fall line with your weight placed evenly between your two skis.

Although essential in the absence of viable alternatives, you are probably finding the snow plough barely adequate to cope with these problems at the increased speeds that now characterize your skiing. It's time to look for new solutions.

Short Turns

On a gentle slope, traverse at not more than about twenty degrees from the fall line. Using the down-up action, make a narrow stem turn to the opposite traverse, finishing at a similarly small angle from the fall line, your skis having turned through forty degrees or less. Now turn back to the original track; turn again; and again. Be sure to accomplish the last part of each turn with the parallel swing of both skis that generates that pleasing grating sound in the snow. And use your poles.

Now link these turns through a continuous down-up rhythm, each downward movement incorporating pole plant and stem, each upward movement embracing a mini-turn with its parallel swing. As soon as you get the rhythm, progress to steeper slopes. Your body is heading directly down the fall line but your speed is being controlled by the extent of edging applied during each parallel swing. Don't swing your body; from the waist upwards you should remain as nearly as possible facing straight down the hill. The change from one traverse body position to the other is sufficient to change your weight distribution and your ski angle, but you need the down-up action each time to achieve the change effectively.

Once this is mastered you can control your speed on those narrow trails without snow ploughing. You can also divide your mountain skiing into sections of traversing and sections of controlled fall line descent.

Stopping from the Schuss

You remember how you stopped yourself on a traverse—by bobbing down and up, swinging your heels on the upward movement? The more pronounced your traverse was across the fall line, the easier it was to stop, because quite a small change in ski direction pointed them up the hill. Now experiment traversing fast, on a gentle slope but close to the fall line. Bob down and up; swing your skis hard through about eighty degrees and edge fiercely. This time it's not so much the turning of your skis across the fall line that is stopping you as the braking effect of your edges in the snow. More of your weight than ever will be thrown against the downhill ski and your body has to angulate to an exaggerated version of the traverse position—legs braced at an angle to control the edged skis while the upper half of the body reaches forward to keep weight on the downhill ski. Do not stick your bottom out as this shifts your weight too far back and your skis may be pressed out in front of you. Practise this from both traverses, slowly increasing your speed on the run-up and reducing the angle from the fall line.

Once this movement can be performed with confidence it is a simple matter to adapt it to the schuss. With your weight distributed evenly, ski straight down the fall line. When you want to stop, decide whether you are going to turn your skis left or right, bob down and swing, stretching your legs as you do so. Performed beautifully, this action is a stop christie. Your stopping power is vastly superior to any snow plough and as your edges bite they sometimes throw snow ahead of you. It is the quintessence of arrogance and bad manners to ski fast towards a group of your friends at the bottom of the slope, stopping dramatically a yard short of collision and in the process showering them with snow. But sometimes it is quite irresistible.

37

Side-Slipping

When traversing, particularly on steeper slopes, it is sometimes useful to be able to lose height without making endless zig-zags and turns, and once in a while some obstacle forces you to take evading action by the same means. By side-slipping you can combine your traverse with controlled slipping down the slope.

All you have to do is reduce the edging on your skis until—more or less flat on the surface of the snow—they begin to slide. By keeping most of your weight on the downhill ski, and by leaning well out from the hill, your stability will be maintained. It helps to lower your body position a little as you slip. Control the speed and extent of this form of descent with your edges and by pressing with your heels. Be careful to keep your downhill pole out of the way. If, in the sideslip, this pole catches the snow, the chances are that it will dig in. Next thing you'll know your skis are hard up against it, bringing your feet to an abrupt halt. Your body may then continue on its downhill course—head first.

You can affect changes in the direction of your sideslip by shifting your weight forward or backwards. With weight back and your edges released, your tails will descend more quickly than your tips. If you start without forward movement, a backward lean can enable you to sideslip with a rearward motion. With weight forward and your edges released, your skis will start to turn towards the fall line. From a vertical sideslip without forward movement, such a weight shift enables you to slip with a forward as well as sideways motion. From the traverse, the release of edges combined with forward lean can be used to initiate a turn.

Survival Skiing

If you find yourself on a descent that exceeds your capacity to turn, and which threatens injury if you try and fail (because of rocks or whatever), you can use side-slipping traverses and link them by kick turns. This is hardly accomplished skiing but, let's face it, you are not an expert yet. It's called *Survival Skiing* and it enables you to enjoy ALL your holiday.

Occasional recourse to survival skiing notwithstanding, your abilities to traverse, stem turn, make short turns straight down the fall line, and to stop suddenly from the schuss add up to *Proper Skiing*. You might quite happily ski like this indefinitely, and many recreational skiers do. But having progressed this far so quickly, your urge for perfection will not let you rest.

Why?

Why, in contrast to what we have seen in the box on page 30, does a forward lean during sideslipping tend to bring skis into the fall line?

Because *when edges are released* the resistance (R) to descent down the slope is centred under the skier's feet, and displacement of the body forward causes the force down the slope (P) to form a rotating force with R, swinging the tips downhill.

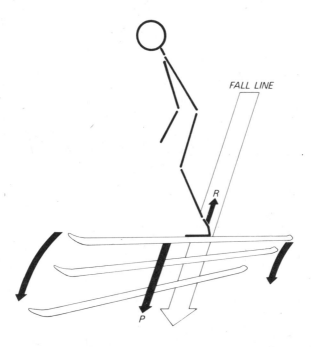

FALL LINE

R

P

A backward lean with edges released has the opposite effect. P moves rearward of R, forcing the tails towards the fall line.

MORE TERMS

OUTSIDE (or INSIDE) SKI

refers to the ski on the outside (or inside) of a turn.

POLE PLANT

the action of reaching forward with either arm (usually the downhill arm) and sticking the point of the pole into the snow (usually so that the skier can turn around it).

SIDE SLIP

the action of releasing edges so that skis slip sideways down the slope.

STEM TURN

a turn in which the uphill ski is stemmed and the other ski is brought parallel to it so that the action is completed parallel.

STEM CHRISTIE

a development of the stem turn in which down-up unweighting allows the un-weighted ski to be brought parallel early in the manoeuvre so that most of the turn is made with skis parallel.

STOP CHRISTIE

a parallel swing of the skis across the direction of travel (uphill, if descent is not down the fall line) bringing the skier abruptly to a stop.

SURVIVAL SKIING

getting down the mountain in one piece without over-much regard for style.

Thinking

I ended my initial fortnight of skiing weighed down by a sense of inadequacy. The pleasing progress of my first week had not been repeated in my second (due in part to wrenching my ankle in a fall). I had not broken through to that happy stage when fun exceeds trepidation; and I had caught myself falling with insufficient cause in the manner condemned in the box on page 35. Nevertheless I had the bug and I determined to do better the next year. While I waited, I thought about skiing.

Come the next season I was able to put on skis and, at my first attempt, ski a simple slope non-stop without falling. My ability and my confidence had improved vastly since my previous contact with snow. By thinking about my lessons and my experience all through those eleven ski-less months I had conditioned my mind to accept such unpalatable necessities as leaning out from the hill and thus to co-operate more fully with my bodily efforts. Before the first week of my second season was over, I was up and away.

The stem christie performed in your imagination, with down-up unweighting, shift of your weight to the outside ski, angulation and so on, can really profit your skiing next time.

Chapter III

Skiing Beautifully

HOW FAR ARE WE GOING?

This book is an introduction to skiing and the scope of this section is limited. My purpose is to whet your appetite and start you on the right lines to ski beautifully. By this I mean skiing parallel, accurately and safely, in a manner that looks effortless and neat. When you have made progress in this direction, but still have a long way to go, you have caught up with me. As I said in my Foreword, now's the time to consult an expert.

No two experts will give the same advice. Schools, styles, fashions and personal flairs favour different methods. Furthermore, fresh experience and improved equipment make for dynamic change so a particular expert may not even give you the same advice two seasons running. The contents of this section are less detailed than hitherto: to fill out the details, find yourself the best available expert and try his panacea.

You have broken through to proper skiing; that took guts. Learning to ski beautifully will call for determination too. Because your confidence and technique have robbed skiing of its terrors, you can enjoy every moment on the slopes, which can easily induce an idle or complacent attitude. You may delude yourself into thinking that continued satisfaction can be obtained by muddling through as a middling skier. Wrong. Skiing is nothing if it is not sensual: the thrill is physical and is brought about by meeting with your ski-borne body the challenge of perfection on the slopes. Nowhere is there a plateau of adequate achievement upon which you may comfortably rest, with or without laurels. So crank up your boots another notch, adjust your bindings, point your skis straight down the hill—and GO!

PARALLEL TURNS

Skis are designed for directional stability. The groove let into the sole of each ski helps ensure that the long, straight boards track accurately across the snow in the direction they are pointing. Moreover, during most of our skiing we are using our edges to improve stability (for instance when traversing) and in so doing we cut little steps in the snow which tend to lock our skis against change of direction. All this directional stability is indispensable to our general welfare on the slopes, but it does pose problems when we want to change direction, that is to say, turn.

So far we have overcome the problem by stemming. First, in the snow plough turn, we stemmed both skis, applied weight to one of them, and found that this induced a turn in the opposite direction. Next, in the stem christie, we stemmed the uphill ski only and at the same time bobbed down. Then, as the stemmed ski began to carry us into our turn, we stretched upwards, bringing the other ski alongside the one carrying our weight, and completed the turn parallel. In both methods we overcame directional stability—the natural tendency to go on forever the way we are pointing—by pushing a ski across the line of flight and transferring weight onto it, so that a new direction was established.

If it's parallel turns we're after, the problem to be overcome is simply this—how to induce a turn without stemming. There are two principal methods, each with many variations. The first employs the down-up action and changes the direction of your skis while they are unweighted; the second uses a combination of edging and reversed bottom camber to curve skis in the desired direction.

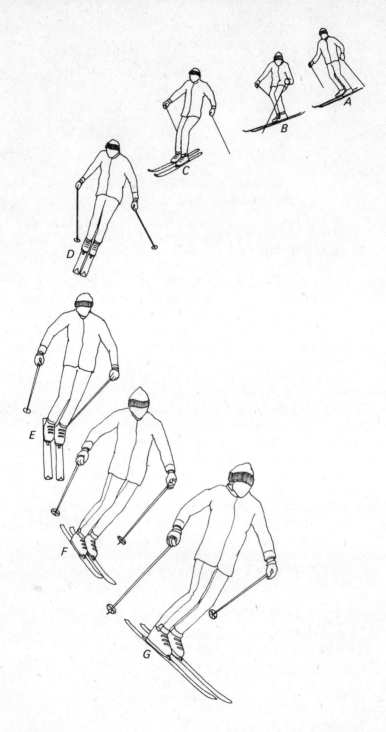

Skidded Parallels

Skidded parallel turns use the unweighting method. The turn starts from a traverse, A, and is similar in many respects to the method of stopping described on page 37. Both arms should be forward and wide of the body, the downhill arm leading. Bend the knees and plant the downhill pole when you reach your lowest 'down' position, B. For a wide turn on a gentle slope plant your pole close to your ski; for a tighter turn on a steeper gradient plant your pole further out.

Immediately after pole-plant, stretch upwards to unweight your skis, C, at the same time pressing down on the pole to get additional lift. Now is your moment to induce the turn, D. Do this by rotating your skis towards the desired direction by a locking movement of the ankles. Usually it is the tails that are skidded outwards from the turn to get the movement started. At the same time that you rotate, change edges and shift weight to the outside ski, E. Your inside ski should now be in the lead, F. Push outwards with the hips and knees to angulate your body from the edged skis in a somewhat exaggerated version of the traverse position, G. When your turn has taken you onto your new traverse, resume straight tracking until you are ready to make your next turn, in the opposite direction.

Skidded parallel turns, well executed, are true Christianias: skiers are frequently content with this method of turning, which can be smooth and graceful. There is, however, another method, smoother and more graceful, which is also more efficient, safer and less tiring. When you are proficient at skidded turns you will of course want to master it. It involves carving our turns.

Why?

Why does the down-up action help one to turn?

Because this unweights our skis, and unweighted skis can be skidded into a new direction relatively easily. But there's more to unweighting than that.

Here's what actually happens to our weight (1) on the skis during a single down-stretch...

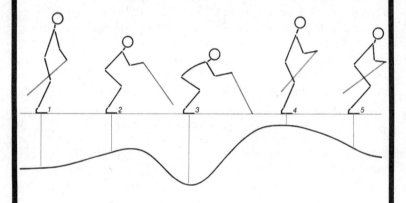

Note that, as you bob down (2), there is a brief moment of unweighting ('down unweighting'); then, as your body reaches its lowest position (3) you apply maximum pressure (useful in carved turns, and on ice); finally, as you stretch upwards (4) you enjoy the longest and most effective period of relative weightlessness ('up unweighting') before normality (5) returns. Remember it is *movement* that affects our weight on the skis, not any static position.

In describing the 'skidded' parallel turn on page 45 I have recommended the moment of up unweighting for inducing a change in ski direction. It is also possible to make use of the down unweighting at the start of the turn to shift your tails laterally.

Carved Parallels

When I had been skiing more or less parallel for a season I began to discover that the more I angulated my body and edged my skis, the easier and more enjoyable turning became. 'I am skiing with my whole body,' I would say, but friends shook their heads sadly. Then, in the chalet, I found what I was groping towards: a clear explanation of the carving turn by the American ski teacher and writer, Warren Witherell. I was on the right track and with the benefit of his article my skiing was transformed. In the carved turn neither of the two major turning forces in a skidded turn is brought to bear. Ski tails are not displaced sideways while unweighted, and friction under the front sections of the skis is not used to produce a turning moment about the balls of the feet (see Box on page 23).

Instead, carving employs the second basic principle for inducing a parallel turn. The side cut of the outside ski is utilized in such a way that a combination of edging and weighting (to produce reverse bottom camber) turns that ski into a crescent-shaped skid that steers you smoothly round your turn. This is how it is done.

Start the turn from a traverse and, initially at any rate, find an easy open slope where you can safely ski fairly fast. Plant your pole merely to trigger the turn, but do not lean upon it. Do not at this stage lower your body as no up unweighting is required. Instead, thrust your knees away from the hill, as it were, into the valley: this has the effect of rolling your ankles, boots and skis towards the fall line and switches your skis from the edges on which you have been traversing onto their opposite edges. Progressively transfer your weight onto the outside (at this stage, still the 'uphill') ski and angulate your body in the appropriate direction. You will start to turn once your skis are edged steeply enough and your angulation is sufficient to force that outside, weighted ski into reverse camber. Advance the inside ski into the lead. Now that convex outside ski will smoothly take control of your steering—carrying you round the turn—instead of being dragged reluctantly onto a new course as in a skidded turn. When you reach the point where you need to shorten the radius of your turn, bend your knees and drop your hip further. This is to achieve the maximum pressure and tighten the arc made by the ski. Throughout the turn keep your body erect, arms wide of the trunk in a position to provide optimum balance.

To summarize, induce the carved turn by changing edges and angulation for the direction required; tighten the turn by additional angulation, bobbing down to increase reverse camber; forget about unweighting and avoid skidding.

The Carved Turn

Carving your turns is remarkably like making turns in an aeroplane: unless you bank you will never get round, and if you go too slowly you may stall. The banking is achieved by edging: you can only ski with sharply edged skis if your speed conjures up sufficient centripetal force for the angulation required. The same simile tells us, accurately, that the faster or sharper you turn, the more banking you need. Just as an aircraft's banked wings prevent it from skidding outwards during a turn, so your edged skis provide the same stability for you.

What?

What is reverse camber? Imagine a ruler 'edged' at 45° to a table top.

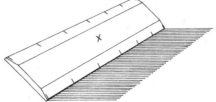

The whole of its edge is in contact with the table-top and no amount of pressure at the centre, 'X', is likely to cause the ruler to bend.

Now suppose we pare away the edge, leaving the ends untouched but progressively reducing the ruler's width towards the centre.

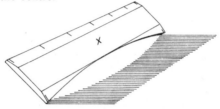

The only points of contact are the two ends. So if pressure is applied at 'X' the ruler will bend until the curved edge again makes contact throughout its length.

Viewed from above, a ski is wide at the shovel, narrow at the waist and broad again at the tail. Between points 'A' and 'B' its edges resemble our pared-down ruler. This sketch exaggerates the proportions.

Edged at forty-five degrees, the ski would make contact with the snow only at points 'A' and 'B', were it not for the skier's weight pressing at 'X', which bends the ski into *reverse camber* and thus forces the curved edge into uniform contact between 'A' and 'B'. This produces a ski bent into the desired curve which carries the 'carving' skier effortlessly round his turn.

You do not abandon skidded turns after you have mastered the carved variety: you need both. There are many slopes where you need to lose speed on your turns, and many crises when you must turn incredibly quickly—usually in such cases the skid is helpful. There are also turns such as the so-called Jet Turn which begins with skis skidded into a new direction during rapid up-unweighting but which continues by a reliance on edging and angulation to achieve carving. Having said that, a mastery of the art of carving opens up a whole new dimension in the joy of skiing and is well worth striving for.

SKIING DEEP POWDER

No Piste for the Wicked

Everything said so far has applied to skiing on pistes, the selected open areas or trails where the snow has been beaten flat by snow cats and myriad skiers. Such surfaces offer fast downhill skiing with sure control for those who know what they're doing. Away from the pistes, on slopes untouched by human ski, lie the vast wonderlands of deep powder.

At least if you're lucky they do. As powder skiing has returned to popularity (and time was when it was *the* respectable form of skiing, vastly to be preferred by skiers of good taste to the new-fangled fad of piste-bashing) off-piste snow is apt to be criss-crossed by thousands of ski trails and punctuated by great holes where luckless, tumbled skiers have floundered for ages trying to recover skis, poles, goggles, equilibrium and dignity. So really you need fresh powder snow, or a helicopter to get you to some virgin area beyond the reach of us poor wingless mortals. A word of warning at the outset—ski off the piste only with the guidance of an instructor or authorized local guide, and then always in a group. Careless invasion of deep snow regions can cause snowslides.

Deep powder is to the piste what gliding is to powered flight. At some sacrifice of speed and versatility, the powder skier enjoys a freedom and oneness with nature that the piste skier cannot experience.

Here's How

Stand on your skis on deep powder. You sink in, perhaps four or five inches. At this depth your weight has compressed the snow sufficiently to support you. If you ski with your skis at the same angle as the slope, as you would do on a piste, your tips will quickly dig deeper into the powder snow and you will describe a parabola. It'll take you some while to get back on your feet and brush some of the snow off your clothes by which time you will probably have figured out what I am going to tell you now. Ski with your tips just above the snow level, which means lowering your centre of gravity and shifting your weight back a little. A popular method is to lean backwards sufficiently to raise the tips, while reaching forward with the arms as a kind of counter-balance.

If you have reached a happily confident stage in your piste skiing your first venture into the powder is likely to surprise you. It feels just exactly as though you had never skied in your life before. The sensation is as delightful as it is bewildering so don't be put off, simply be prepared for an altogether new experience.

You would do well to plan a modest initial venture—say, out into the powder for a couple of hundred metres of traverse, a turn, and back to the piste further down. Survive this and you'll have the confidence and urge to try more. Basic rules are: weight both skis evenly for normal running, including the traverse; keep your skis parallel and as close together as possible; increase slightly the lead of your uphill ski. If you find your traverse too fast, just increase the weight on your downhill ski and this will turn you gently into the hill till you stop. Weighting your uphill ski will have the opposite effect and you can if you like make your first turn in deep powder simply by shifting your weight in this manner. You will turn remarkably quickly, so be ready to return your weight evenly between both skis as soon as you are onto your new traverse.

Once you gain confidence you will find the braking effect of deep powder tempts you, except on the steepest slopes, to ski more or less down the fall line. Speed is controlled by turns across the fall line, rather like the linked christies used to the same effect on the piste. Keep your skis parallel and close together and try to achieve a slow motion bounce rhythm in which you sink back on your skis, then, as you plant your pole, spring upwards with an exaggerated up motion that banks your body towards the pole—in the direction of the turn. This banking will guide your skis, which have been lifted momentarily by your strong up action, into their new course. As you sink back on your skis you are making the down action for the next bounce. Each bounce switches you from one side of the fall line to the other. Instead of skidding your tails you are in effect lifting your tips and turning them into the new direction.

Changing Styles

Be ready to change stance and style quickly as you leave the piste for the powder and on your return. This involves shifting your weight back and getting your tips up on entering the powder, and leaning forward with edges correctly set the moment you are back on the hardpack.

ICE

My first skiing holiday was not under ideal conditions and in his search for parts of the valley which hadn't returned to verdant cow pastures our instructor took us ever higher up north-facing slopes, so that we found ourselves practising our snow plough turns at the top of what to me seemed great slabs of ice propped up against mountains at 45 degrees. Ghastly though this seemed at the time, it has had the effect of making all subsequent ski experience on actual *snow* seem heavenly, and, paradoxically, it left me strangely confident that I could handle ice.

In fact any skier's ability to ski on ice rests almost entirely on confidence. There is ice and ice, ranging from *blue ice* of the skating rink variety, which almost no one likes, to *grey ice,* solid and slippery, but manageable, down to *frozen granular ice,* which has the lowest water content of the three and presents a crunchy surface for your edges to bite into.

Faced with a limited area of blue ice, try to avoid enterprising manoeuvres until you have crossed it. In all other ice conditions, perform normally, with economy of motion and maximum uniformity of pressure on the edges. By all means ski with a wider than usual gap between your skis. If slipping occurs, do not panic—that way you are bound to fall—but edge more sharply, lower your body to achieve temporary increased weight along the edges, and adjust your angulation for balance. Turns that are carved present edged skis to the surface and are less vulnerable to slipping on ice than skidded turns where the skis are more nearly flat on the surface.

More often than not it is the unforeseen, sudden transition from snow to ice that (in more than one meaning of the word) throws people. Anticipation, that essential element in all advanced skiing, combined with determination not to be cheated, provides the best defence. I had something to say early in this book about confidence. Now that you are skiing rather well, here's my last word on that subject.

A skier needs confidence to improve, and each achievement feeds his confidence. But he never needs the type of confidence that tells him he knows it all, or which makes him believe that nothing untoward is ever liable to happen.

MOGULS

The Problem

The multitude of skiers on modern ski slopes, all turning, edging and gouging the snow with their skis as they make their way from top to bottom, achieve one side effect that has altered the whole sport of skiing. They create moguls.

Moguls are most likely to be found on frequently skied, steep sections of the piste where skiers have to turn most often and most sharply and where snow cats cannot easily bash the surface flat again. What is a mogul? It is a hard packed mound of snow. And where there is one mogul there are usually a hundred, separated only by evil-looking valleys—often more than a metre below the surrounding summits.

Like deep powder and ice, moguls can seem more difficult to master than they are. In fact, given the correct technique and practice, crashing through a field of moguls can be a fun sport in its own right. But the sport can be testing, not to say exhausting, and deserves careful study and application.

The Individual Mogul

Practise skiing over an isolated mogul (a sharp bump or ridge will do for this exercise). If you allow your whole body to rise up by the height of the obstacle, if in other words you hold a normal skiing position, you are likely to become airborne on the far side. Fine if you are practising a jump, but hopeless for coping with moguls—because on the real slope there are dozens more ahead of you. So, as your skis ride up over the bump, allow your body position to become compressed, knees driven up almost to the chest, into a squatting stance.

Once the full height of the mogul has been 'swallowed' in this way, ensure continued contact between skis and snow by immediately extending your legs, thus reverting to a normal ski position. To achieve all this you need to approach the bump with your hips slightly behind your heels. Not too far, for obvious reasons, but a forward lean is liable to lead to contact between knee and chin at the high point of the swallow. This 'swallowing' technique is called body compression or *avalement*.

Avalement with Turn

Ski tactics in a mogul field will require constant changes in direction while you soak up the individual bumps by the body compression method. The turn is best made while your skis are immediately over the highest part of the mogul, at which split second the only contact should be the inch or two of soles directly beneath your boots. By cranking your knees in the direction of turn, and assisting with foot twist, your skis will swivel easily to the new direction. As you descend on the far side, your edges must be set appropriately. Remember to keep the skis in contact with the surface as much as possible. Pole plant helps anchor the upper part of the body and actuates the ski swivel and edge change.

Avalement with Turn

Sometimes you will cross a mogul about half or two thirds up its height, leaving the summit to one side. You can easily turn as it were around the contours of that mogul, with its summit on the inside of your turn, but by avoiding the summit you deprive yourself of the opportunity of turning in the opposite direction. If the shape of a valley permits it, a turn can be made between moguls.

The Mogul Field

A great deal of practice is needed on relatively easy bumps and over small groups of bumps before you can ski fast and without upset through the most difficult fields. You must 'swallow' the bumps and you must be capable of accurate timing to achieve your turns at the most advantageous points in your crossings. When you tackle 20, 40, 100 consecutive moguls, your mind must plan ahead to decide your route over, between and round the moonscape ahead of you while at the same time sending those rapid orders to your body for the negotiation of the particular brute now forcing your knees up in front of your face. Like I said earlier, fun: exhausting fun.

AVALEMENT

compressing the body by bringing knees up almost to the chest, into a squatting stance. Also known as 'swallowing' a mogul.

CENTRIPETAL FORCE

a force drawing a body to a centre. In some skiing turns centripetal force creates a need for a skier to adjust his balance by leaning toward the centre of the turn.

CUT OF THE SKI

the relative dimensions of the shovel, waist and tail of a ski when viewed from above. Otherwise known as side camber.

MOGUL

a hard-packed mound of snow.

MOGUL FIELD

an area covered with adjacent moguls.

PARALLEL TURN

a turn during which the skis remain parallel. Also known as a Christiania. Parallel turns may be 'skidded' or 'carved'.

SHOVEL

the broader front section of a ski when viewed from above.

SNOW CAT

a machine on tracks with rollers to flatten out the piste.

WAIST

the narrow centre section of a ski when viewed from above.

Chapter IV

Et Cetera

MANNERS

Behaviour on Skis

So far in this book I have written as though you were the only skier in sight. Unhappily this will seldom be so. Collision is a real danger which can lead to nasty injuries.

Ski under control: this is the *first basic rule*. Be aware of other skiers on the slope. Check traffic before starting, including a look uphill for on-coming skiers.

Second basic rule: when you are overtaking, you are responsible for avoiding skiers below or beyond you. Even if such skiers make sudden turns or whatever, the responsibility for avoiding collision is entirely yours. As you approach, let the skier downhill of you know which side you are coming: 'passing right', etc.

Third basic rule: look before turning. Get into this habit early in your training and never abandon it: it will spare you from otherwise inevitable prangs, and save you from slobs who ignore basic rules No. 1 and 2. Ski defensively.

When approaching another skier on an opposite traverse, pass to the right. If you enter a main piste from a small trail, give way. Give inexperienced or nervous skiers a wide berth. Remember how you felt not so long ago! Do not bomb down the slope between an instructor and his class.

At the top of a lift and at the bottom of a piste, get clear quickly to make room for those following. If you stop during a descent (and you are made of sterner stuff than I am if you do not), pull off to the edge of the trail. Follow posted instructions at lifts and on slopes. Study the chart of pistes and trails and choose sensibly.

Whenever possible (and invariably in fog, very cold temperatures, off piste or on an unfamiliar trail) ski with one or more companions. To be gloomy but realistic, you could die from exposure if you suffered an incapacitating injury or equipment failure, or got lost, on your own. Stop skiing when you are really tired and avoid poor visibility skiing whenever you can.

Behaviour off Skis

When you carry your skis over your shoulder, be careful not to swing them round horizontally as you turn, swiping those beside you. Raise them nearly vertical first, then turn.

Wait your turn in lift queues. You may have to accept, with however much ill grace, line cutting by instructors, officials and, occasionally, authorized teams and classes. Do not accept queue-barging by others who have no authority, however young they may be or however strong their accents. Did you imagine your ski poles were just for balance? There is a whole sub-sport devoted to keeping the insolent and arrogant in their proper places in the queue. Use your imagination, cunning and of course ski poles. Some folk need good manners thrusting upon them: they'll be grateful to you ten years hence.

Remember what was said early in this book about taking care never to allow a ski to career downhill on its own. Place skis flat to fit them, and attach safety straps. Some centres allow, instead of straps, devices called ski stoppers. These are hinged retarding spikes which spring out at ninety degrees to the ski when the boot and binding part.

Don't play the fool on lifts by swinging chairs or bouncing on buttons, or whatever. Keep poles tucked in (and skis too, if carried) to avoid snarling uprights. If skis are worn on a chair lift, keep the tips up at take off and when approaching the landing strip.

EMERGENCIES

Avalanches

An avalanche or snow slip represents the most severe hazard to life among skiers. As a recreational skier your safety is largely in the hands of the ski centre staff, who are responsible for restricting skiing to safe areas. Obey such restrictions carefully and do not venture off the marked piste without the guidance of an instructor or authorized local guide.

Injuries

It's no good pretending you are never going to see someone hurt skiing. Sooner or later one of your group, or someone just ahead of you on the piste, is going to fall and not get up, and you and your friends are going to have to do something about it. Something helpful, let's hope.

Now, most ski centres have stretcher sleighs at convenient points on the slopes, often at the tops of lifts where trained patrolmen are working. Telephones connect tops and bottoms of lifts. If the injured skier cannot complete the descent, probably the best solution is to organize a stretcher sleigh recovery.

Make the victim comfortable and warm, as protection against shock as much as against exposure, without causing unnecessary movement if a fracture is suspected. Cross a pair of skis upright in the snow uphill of him or her. One of you should stay with the injured person while others ski down to the bottom of the lift (or wherever help can be found) to report the *exact* location of the accident. A telephone call, and the stretcher sleigh is on its way. In at least one country which will not be named, the stretcher party may refuse to rescue the injured person until paid for the service, so either have money or friends. Behaviour of this sort seems pretty soulless to me, but that's how people get rich.

APRÈS SKI

No, I'm not going to tell you what and what not to do *après* ski. Some people endure skiing as a kind of penance entitling them to the fun that comes after; others save their money and their energy for an extra day on the slopes. You pays your money. . . .

As a beginner you are vulnerable to the chalet bore. Aware that, in the Land of the Blind the One-Eyed is King, this sportsman is ever ready to impress the unfortunate newcomer with stories and advice. Listen, if no polite alternative occurs to you, but don't be overawed. More important, don't be misled by skiing hints that belong to the age of wooden skis, bamboo poles, Kandahar bindings and lace-up leather boots. Skiing was a very different sport fifteen years ago and all sorts of special skills were needed to turn those enormously long skis, attached relatively loosely to supple boots. Many of those skills are unwanted today, as modern equipment makes new demands and calls for different techniques.

BUYING EQUIPMENT

One ski magazine I read devotes three long articles each season to evaluating skis. Further space is devoted to boots, bindings and other paraphernalia of that very big sales business—ski equipment. If you have ever ventured into the worlds of hi-fi or wine-drinking or, dare I say it, choosing a package holiday, you know what to expect: a dazzling kaleidoscope of plus features, exclusive offers and fantastic value for money provided you can afford to pay. It's all here too, with just the same imponderables until it's too late; until you've bought your gear and you either like it or you don't.

My advice is simple. Rent while you are a beginner; rent again the second season, but this time taking as much care in choosing as though you were buying, and swopping mid-holiday if you are less than completely satisfied. Buy, if you want to buy, at the tail end of that season when the stores are offering huge discounts. (The retail mark-up on ski equipment is enormous and you should avoid paying anything like list prices.) Base your choice on all the advice you can muster but finally on your own proven preference. Aim off for your enhanced ability in the years ahead but only buy the absolute Olympic range if you really are that good or if you really need to feel that good, and can afford to pander to that kind of feeling. But don't waste your money buying rubbish: better to go on renting good gear. Remember good bindings will save you from injury on second-rate skis, but the reverse is not the case. Do make sure your boots fit both your feet and your bindings, the latter being adjustable to ensure proper attachment and correct release. The Ski Club of Great Britain offers expert and impartial advice on ski equipment. Finally, if you do buy your own equipment, have it correctly maintained and checked out before each new season.

PHYSICAL FITNESS

I deliberately left this nearly to the end. Most ski books put it first, where it rightly belongs, but where it casts a melancholy shadow across the happy sport of skiing. Yes, of course you need to be reasonably fit, and the fitter you are when you start, the less crippling you will find your lessons, and the more you will learn and enjoy. But we are not in the business of training Alpine Commandos or even coaching Olympic champions (not yet, anyway): we are concerned with breaking through initiation and second-year classes into the realm of sheer enjoyment. So get yourself as fit as you reasonably can by fifteen minutes of exercise each day for, say, a month before your holiday.

Exercises should:

1 Warm you up—body stretching; head-roll; shoulder relaxing; toe touching.
2 Exercise your abdomen—sit-ups and leg raising from lying on your back.
3 Likewise exercise your back—on stomach with feet braced; lift arms and chest away from floor.
4 Strengthen your legs—running upstairs or up hills; stepping on and off a bench 15–20 inches high; hopping over a bar 10–12 inches high, with feet together, apart or jumping from one to the other; jumping on toes; skipping; bouncing in crouched position, followed by jump to extend legs.
5 Exercise your arms and shoulders—push-ups; rope climbing.

COMPETITIVE SKIING

Even at an early stage, it's fun to test your ability against your chums and your instructor may organize simple races. Some ski schools encourage pupils to qualify for proficiency awards by skiing against a standard set by the chief instructor. For the experts, events are in three categories—Slalom, Downhill and Giant Slalom.

Slalom

Racers pass through a series of gates, each marked by two flags of the same colour. Gates are numbered and there may be forty or more of them. Gates may be 'open' horizontal to the fall line or 'closed', vertically arranged. Double gates consist of two gates together, set parallel to one another either obliquely to the slope or vertically down it. A *salvis* is a pair of closed (vertical) gates; *enfilades,* a vertical line of closed gates; a *chicane* is a series of vertical gates set in a slightly oblique line; and a *seelos* is a group of three gates, the first being open, the second closed, and the third open.

In Slalom, turning fast and accurately is the thing. There is hardly a pause between gates.

Downhill

Hold your breath and don't panic. I mean just watching 'em. The Downhill Race consists simply of tearing down a clearly marked piste at least twenty metres wide which is sufficiently free of sharp bends that competitors can race without using their poles to turn. Frequently they adopt the 'egg' position—a crouching stance designed to reduce wind resistance—and hold it as they hurtle down the course, except when carving their way round turns with angulation and reverse camber to help them. Competitors start at intervals and are racing against the clock.

If ever you reach the point where your skiing seems rather good, to you that is, go and watch a downhill race. To have your ego completely shattered, watch the local kids' team go.

Giant Slalom

This event is something of a mixture of Downhill and Slalom. The course may be between 2–3 kilometers long with 300–600 meters (1–2000 feet) height loss between start and finish. Such a course might have 30 to 50 gates, at least six meters apart placed on the piste which is about 30 meters wide. The vertical or closed gates may be passed through from either side.

Epilogue

I started writing this book at the end of my second European skiing holiday, worked on it through two full ski seasons in Iran, and am finishing it back here in England. My aim throughout has been to describe each movement while the experience of learning it was still vividly remembered. Reading the early paragraphs again now I have to resist a temptation to remove evidence of my own slow and painful initiation: such editing would, it seems to me, destroy much of the book's value. This remains to the end a book about skiing by a non-expert skier, conscious of the ignorance, apprehension and controlled excitement shared by all beginners when they fit skis to boots for the first time.

If my words help you to enjoy skiing as much as I enjoy skiing, that's good.

INDEX TO SKI TERMS

(Definitions are found on the pages listed.)